THE NATIONAL TRUST

Investigating

THE
SEASHORE

By Gillian Osband
Illustrated by David Simonds

Contents

The seashore 2
Rocks, minerals and fossils 4
Seashore plants 6
Animals which look like plants 8
Spiny-skinned animals 9
Seashore worms 10
Animals in armour 11
Animals which live in shells 12
Seashore fish 14
Seashore birds 16
Marine mammals 20
The seashore at work 22
Danger! 25
Defence 26
Smugglers 28
Seaside holidays 30
Pollution 31
Answers 32

Sponsored by

Kellogg's

The seashore

As soon as you arrive at the seashore you know that you have entered a different world. Sniff the salty air, listen to the waves pounding the rocks and watch the sea birds as they swoop through the air. The seashore is an exciting place to be.

This is a world of smugglers and wreckers, fishing and history, holidays and fun. It is also a world of birds, animals, fish and plants waiting to be explored.

Do's and don'ts

The seashore is a wonderful world to explore, but remember it can also be a very dangerous place.

* Tell someone where you are going.

* Make sure you know what time is high tide. In some places the tide comes in very fast, and many small coves and beaches are completely covered. You may set off to explore round some rocks and find you can't get back to the beach.

* Rocks can be slippery. Rock pools can be deeper than they look. Be careful!

* Never try to climb up or down cliffs. Stay away from the cliff edge and keep to the path. If you have a dog, keep it on the lead if you are walking on a cliff top.

* Let someone know if you are going swimming. The sea might look calm, but there may be strong currents. **Never** ignore a sign which says swimming is dangerous.

Enterprise Neptune

This beautiful and exciting place is under threat. Over the years, hundreds of miles of seashore have been ruined forever by pollution, industry and building. That's why, in 1965, the National Trust launched an appeal to save the remaining unspoilt coastline around England, Wales and Northern Ireland. The appeal was named Enterprise Neptune, after the Roman god of the sea, and its target was to save 900 miles of coastline from further development. Twenty-five years later, over 500 miles of endangered coastline have come under the National Trust's care, thanks to the appeal. But there is still a long way to go before Enterprise Neptune reaches its target.

The tides

It won't be long before you notice that the sea regularly comes inland, covering the seashore, and then goes out, uncovering it again. There are usually two low tides and two high tides every twenty-four hours.

The tides rise and fall to the pull of the moon as it waxes (grows bigger) and wanes (becomes a silvery crescent). Twice a month, when the moon is at its fullest and at its thinnest, very high tides called springs occur. Because the moon rises later each day than the day before, the times of the tides also change.

Try to have with you

A pencil, notebook, camera (if you have one), spade, bucket, net and a plastic bag for collecting shells. Buy or borrow a guide to the seashore in the area you're visiting. Every stretch of coastline is different.

3

Rocks, minerals and fossils

Almost all the earth is made up of rocks and minerals. Rocks are often made up of minerals of more than one type. Fossils are the remains of animals and plants, often millions of years old, which have been preserved in rocks.

If you are interested in rocks, minerals and fossils, one of the best places to learn about them is around the coastline.

Stand back and look up at a cliff face. You don't need to be an expert to see that the cliff contains rock stratae (layers) of different ages and types. You should be able to see the different colours and textures of the various stratae. Remember, rock formations will change from area to area.

There are three main kinds of rocks. Here are some for you to look out for in each category.

Igneous: rocks formed by heat action.

Granite – may be pink, brown, grey or yellow
Basalt – very dark, formed from volcanic lava

Sedimentary: rocks formed from sand, shells, dead plants and animals that have been washed down and left on the sea bed in layers. Over a long period of time, the weight of the top layer presses the layer beneath to form rock.

Sandstone – brown, red or yellowish
Limestone – formed under water. Pure limestone is white. Good source of fossils

Metamorphic: began as either igneous or sedimentary rock, but changed into another type of rock as a result of great heat or pressure, with a different structure, and often a different colour.

Slate – heat and pressure on clay can turn it into slate which breaks into smooth, flat sheets of rock. Slates are often used for roofing
Quartzite – a very hard rock formed from sandstone under intense heat

Take a book with you to help you to identify the various rocks and minerals you find. Only collect small pieces of rock and mineral lying on the beach or at the bottom of a cliff. **Never** chip pieces off a cliff or rock face.

Looking for fossils

You are most likely to find fossils in limestone cliffs which are formed from plant, shell and animal remains.

Look carefully where the rock is cut away and the layers have been exposed. Fossils may be embedded in the layers.

Some very impressive fossils have been found in limestone cliffs. In 1811, the first complete fossil of a dinosaur, an Ichthyosaur, was found at Black Venn, near Lyme Regis in Dorset.

You are most likely to find ammonites, trilobites and the outlines of plants preserved in the rock.

Pick up small pieces of limestone or sandstone from the beach and take a good look at them. You might find one with a fossil to add to your rock collection.

Never try to climb a cliff to look at different rock stratae. **Never** break pieces of rock off a cliff face.

Extraordinary names

You will come across some very odd place names around the coast. Try to find out how they got their names.

Ralph's Cupboard, Cornwall
The Giant's Causeway, Northern Ireland
Baggy Point, Devon
Hell's Mouth Bay, Gwynedd
The Dodman, Cornwall

Some places to visit with spectacular rock formations

Cornwall
Crackington Haven – the carboniferous shales here have been pushed into zig-zag folds by movements of the earth's crust, millions of years ago.
Pedn-vounder – the granite here is in blocks, cube piled on cube, like building bricks. You can also see the rocking 66-ton Logan Rock!

Dorset
Charmouth – look carefully at the cliff face and the broken rocks for ammonites and other fossils.
Lulworth – the folded stratae here are the result of the outermost ripples of the great earth movements that formed the Alps millions of years ago.

Isle of Wight
Alum Bay – the multi-coloured sands are famous here, and are part of an important section of stratae from the Tertiary Age.

Northern Ireland
The Giant's Causeway – 60 million years ago, lava poured out through cracks in the earth's surface, and solidified as regular-sided basalt columns. Most of the columns on this stretch of coast are six-sided, but some are four-, five-, seven- or even ten-sided. Many of these formations have been given names, like the Giant's Organ and the Harp. You can easily see why.

South Wales
Gower Peninsula – bones of mammoths, auruchs and bison which roamed the earth thousands of years ago have been found trapped in the sedimentary rocks in this area.

Seashore plants

Seaweeds

Seaweeds are the commonest plants along the seashore. They do not grow like plants on land because they have no real roots. They cling to rocks or to the sea bed with suckers, called holdfasts, and can withstand the force of the tide and waves.

Look for seaweeds:

along the shoreline when the tide goes out
among the rocks
around breakwaters
on the sea bed

Some seaweeds to look for:

Sea lettuce (green)

Jump on a clump of bladder wrack. The loud 'plops' are the sound of the bladders bursting. These bladders act like waterwings, and when filled with air they keep the seaweed afloat in the water. Bladder wrack can grow over three metres long. The pieces you find on the shore have broken off the main plant.

Dulse (deep red)

Knotted wrack (greeny-brown)

Oarweed (brown)

The magic of seaweed

Seaweeds have many uses. Large brown seaweeds contain iodine which is used as an antiseptic. Many varieties of seaweed are used to make natural fertiliser as they contain nitrogen which helps plants to grow. You can even eat some kinds of seaweed such as laverbread and dulse. Crispy seaweed is a popular dish in Chinese restaurants.

Make a seaweed barometer

You can forecast the weather with the help of bladder wrack. Take a piece home and hang it up. When the weather is dry, the seaweed will dry up. When it is going to rain, the seaweed absorbs the moisture from the air and the bladder wrack become moist and plump again.

Make a seaweed collection

Every tide brings in something different. Green seaweeds grow close to the shore and are only covered at high tide. Brown seaweeds are usually found between the tide marks. Red seaweeds grow in deeper waters.

Other seashore plants

Some plants grow well in sand dunes. Others thrive in saltmarsh areas where a river meets the sea and there is a mixture of sand and mud. Some plants even grown in crevices on the cliff face itself.

Some seashore plants to spot

On the sand dunes and shingle

Sea spurge

Prickly saltwort

Yellow-horned poppy

Sea bindweed

Sea kale

Marram grass

On saltmarshes

Sea lavender

Sea milkwort

Sea plantain

On the cliffs

When you see any of these plants, make a note of their colouring and colour these drawings in when you get home.

Thrift

Sea campion

Glasswort

Make a seashore diary

If you are lucky enough to live near the sea, you can visit the seashore through the year and keep a diary of how the animal and plant life changes with the seasons.

If you go on a seaside holiday, make a daily record of everything you see.

You need: a notebook, pencil, crayons, camera (if possible)

Write down the date, the object you found, where and what time of day you found it.

Draw a picture of the object and colour it in. If you have a camera, take a photograph and stick it in your notebook when it has been developed. If you don't recognise what you've found, look it up in a book when you get home and add any interesting facts to your notes.

The cliff code

When you are exploring, remember that cliffs are dangerous. Some paths are on the top of steep cliffs. Keep to the path. Keep your dog on the lead. If you are not walking with your parents, tell someone where you are going.

Animals which look like plants

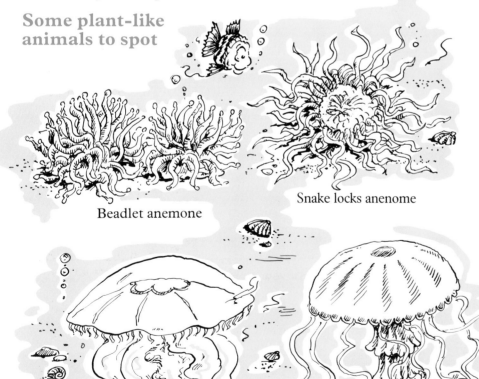

I'M AN ANIMAL!

Explore the rocks, the pools between them and the pools around the timber breakwaters at low tide. Many animals live in these pools. Some may *look* like plants, but they are actually animals.

What is the difference between a plant and an animal?

Animals have to search for their food. Plants get their food from the air, soil, water and sunlight.

Animals stop growing once they have reached a certain size. Many plants die back at certain seasons and then completely re-grow.

Animals have a nervous system responding to touch. This is very rare in plants.

Some plant-like animals to spot

Beadlet anemone

Snake locks anenome

Common jellyfish

Compass jellyfish

Useful facts

Sea anemones are highly coloured and often very beautiful. They are very greedy and use their waving tentacles to sting small animals which they then eat. If you disturb an anemone, it will withdraw its tentacles and look like a coloured stump.

A red jelly-like blob on the side of an exposed rock is a closed anemone waiting for the tide to return and cover it, so that it can start searching for food again.

A jelly-like blob on the beach is a dead jellyfish. If this strange animal gets stranded on the shoreline, the air and sun gradually evaporate the water it contains and it dies.

The constant problem facing all creatures of the shore is how to retain enough water to breathe, and how to avoid drying up when they are uncovered by the ebbing tide. Anemones have an effective line of defence. They fill their stomachs with sea-water, and, if necessary, their outer layer of mucus dries to form a hard crust, retaining water beneath it.

Spiny~skinned animals

Seashore animals have developed various ways of protecting themselves. The members of the echinoderm group have spines. These spines can be in the form of a spike, as with sea urchins, or look like a tiny knob, as with starfish.

Spiny-skinned animals to spot

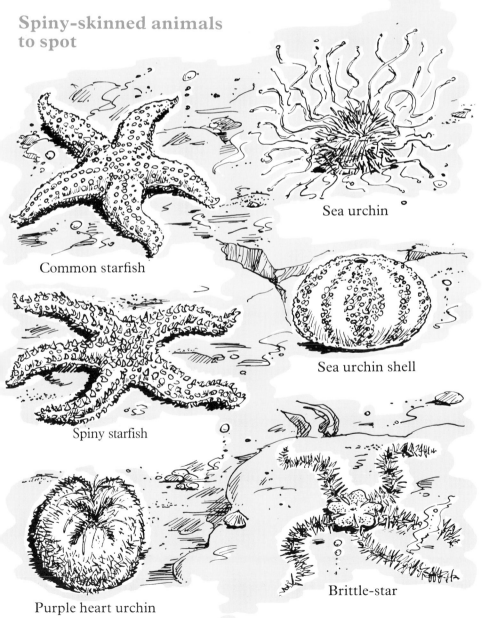

Common starfish

Sea urchin

Sea urchin shell

Spiny starfish

Brittle-star

Purple heart urchin

Starfish

If you find a starfish, pick it up very gently. Run your finger along it. It will feel rough and spiny. You should be able to see the central disc which allows sea water to enter the starfish. Turn the starfish over. Down the centre of each limb is a groove. Look closely, and you will see that each groove is filled with hundreds of little fleshy tubes which act as its feet. These enable the starfish to creep along the beach or sea bed, and are also powerful suckers. They are used to sieze its prey and are even strong enough to prise open shells to eat the animal inside. When you have finished looking at the starfish, put it back where you found it.

Where to look

In rock pools and breakwater pools
Under stones and piles of seaweed
Among the rocks at low tide

Taking photographs

If you have a camera, take photographs of all the interesting things you discover around the shore.

There are many ways you can use these photos when they are developed:
Put them in your seashore record book
Use them as a reference to paint pictures
Make a calendar, using a different photo to decorate each month

9

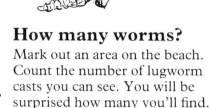

Seashore worms

Seashore worms are probably the commonest animals on the seashore. Some protect themselves by making shell-like coverings out of sand, some burrow in the sand and some crawl along the surface.

How many worms?

Mark out an area on the beach. Count the number of lugworm casts you can see. You will be surprised how many you'll find.

Seashore worms to spot

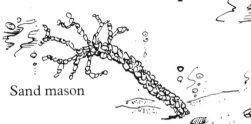

Sand mason

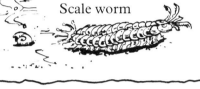

Scale worm

Peacock worm

Did you know?

The bootlace worm is extremely long. It can grow to a length of four metres and gets its name because it is very narrow and looks like a bootlace.

Useful facts

The rag worm has strong jaws and a pair of overlapping claws. If you pick one up, be careful. It might bite you.

The lugworm lives in a U-shaped burrow in the sand. It sucks sand from one end of the burrow and swallows it to digest the tiny particles of food contained in the sand. This causes a constant downflow of sand and leaves a hollow on the surface. The worm passes the 'sieved' sand out through its tail end, forming casts on the surface. You will see these coiled worm casts and small hollows all over sandy beaches. These tell-tale signs mean that lugworms are easy prey for fishermen who use them as fishing bait.

The sand mason is a strange worm. It builds itself a tube-shaped shell out of coarse sand grains and gravel stuck together

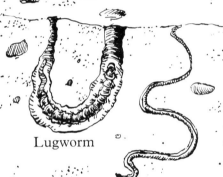

Lugworm

Bootlace worm

with mucus. When the tide comes in, the worm pushes itself to the top of the open tube to gather its food from the water. At low tide it retreats down the tube, well below the opening. Look carefully along the shoreline for these odd-looking 'chimneys', with a frill of sandy threads at their tops.

A seashore scavenger

One of the commonest scavengers of the shore is the sand hopper. It is a cousin of the shrimp but doesn't like swimming. Its nickname is the 'beach flea' because it is such a great jumper.

Who left these marks on the sand?

Answers on page 32

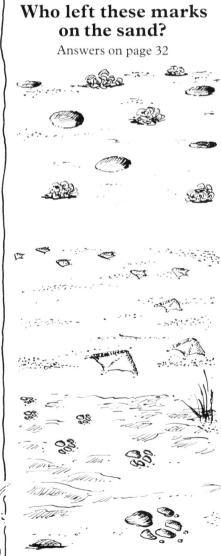

Animals in armour

As the tide goes out you'll see some of the odd creatures that have shells on their backs to protect themselves. These animals are called crustaceans. Their shells are jointed, like medieval armour, so that the animal inside can move its limbs. The shell doesn't grow and is cast off when the animal gets too big for it. It is replaced by a new skin which hardens to form a shell again.

Crustaceans to look out for

Common prawn

Edible crab

Hermit crab

Spider crab

Where to look

On rocks

In rock pools

Under seaweed and rocks

Along the shore

Useful facts

The hermit crab has armour on the front half of its body, but no protection at the back. It protects itself by finding an empty shell and crawls backwards into it. When the hermit crab grows, it finds itself a bigger home. Never try to pull a hermit crab out of its shell.

The spider crab has such thin legs that it cannot travel very fast with its heavy body. To protect itself, it camouflages itself by using bits of seaweed and sponges if it is among plants, and with tiny stones and shells if it is among rocks. Be very careful when looking for this crab, as its legs are easily broken.

Most crabs scuttle sideways when they move. When frightened, some of them retreat backwards.

Large mussels often provide homes for two different crustaceans. Barnacles attach themselves to the outside of mussel shells. There is also space in the mussel shell for the tiny pea crab to live.

Seashore scavenging

As you walk along the shore, or explore among the rocks and rock pools, you will find all sorts of things to collect. Here are a few to look out for: shells, empty crab shells, dead sea urchins and starfish, skate's egg case, egg cluster of a whelk, seaweeds, pieces of sponge, interesting pieces of driftwood, smooth pebbles, pieces of limestone with fossils, pieces of glass rubbed smooth by the sea, washed-up fishing corks, feathers.

Animals which live in shells

You will see shells of all shapes, sizes and colours as you walk along the seashore.

Shells are the homes of creatures called molluscs. When molluscs die, their shells are left empty. Shells in one piece are called univalves and shells in two sections are called bivalves.

Some shells to look for

Univalves:

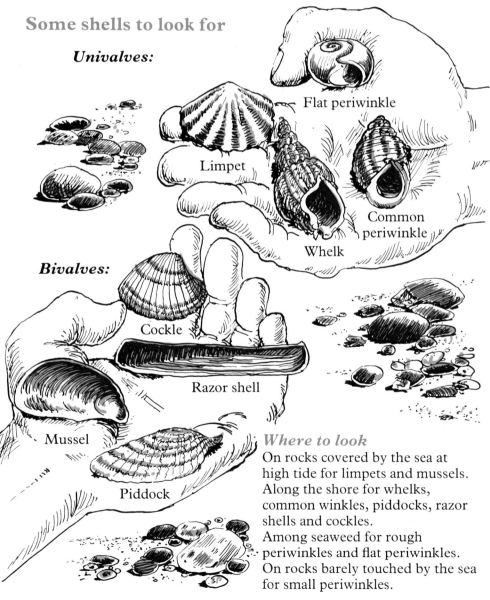

Flat periwinkle

Limpet

Common periwinkle

Whelk

Bivalves:

Cockle

Razor shell

Mussel

Piddock

Where to look
On rocks covered by the sea at high tide for limpets and mussels. Along the shore for whelks, common winkles, piddocks, razor shells and cockles.
Among seaweed for rough periwinkles and flat periwinkles. On rocks barely touched by the sea for small periwinkles.

Useful facts

Univalves crawl around on a single thick foot which looks like a tongue. They have feelers, eye spots and teeth. Some, like whelks, are carnivorous. Others, like periwinkles, are vegetarian.

The limpet clings tightly to the rock it has chosen. It only moves to feed on nearby plants at high tide. A limpet has nearly two thousand teeth!

The whelk is a nasty creature. It eats other molluscs, especially mussels and oysters, by drilling a hole through its victim's shell with its toothed tongue. It then puts its proboscis (which looks like a trunk) into the hole and sucks out the mollusc.

Bivalves do not have teeth. They have two tubes called siphons for feeding. One tube draws in sea-water, the other forces it out. As the water passes through the bivalve, the animal digests the tiny pieces of plant life.

The cockle and razor shell hide themselves by burrowing into the sand. When the tide washes over the sand they push out their siphons in search of food.

When the tide goes out, the periwinkle closes its shell with a horny disc, like closing a door, to keep the moisture inside its shell until the tide comes in again. This 'door' also protects the animal from the prying claws of crabs.

Use your shells to:
Decorate a box
Decorate a hair comb or belt
 buckle
Thread and make
 a necklace

Collecting shells

You need: a small spade, a sieve, plastic bags, a box lined with cotton wool

Try to find clean, unbroken shells of as many different types and colours as possible. Make sure they are all empty. A sieve is useful for uncovering shells in mud or sand, especially tiny ones. Put fragile shells in the box, and the rest in the bags. When you get home, wash them in soapy, warm water. Soak any stained shells in water with a few drops of bleach added to it. Rinse the shells in cold water and leave them to dry.

Make a shell picture

Draw the outline of your design on some thick card, then find shells to fit the drawing and glue them on. Use small shells to fill any awkward shapes.

Seashore fish

Many types of fish only live in the deepest part of the sea, and probably the only time you'll see these is on the fishmonger's slab. However, there are some species of fish which prefer the shallow bays and rocky pools of the seashore.

Some seashore fish to spot

Butterfish

Rock goby

Fifteen-spined stickleback

Shanny

Hooknose

Where to look
In rock pools covered by the tide for the fifteen-spined stickleback, rock goby, butterfish and shanny. In shallow water for the sand eel, lesser weever, young whiting, female mackerel (in the spring, when they swim near the shore to lay their eggs).
In mud and sand where a river meets the sea for the flounder and sole.

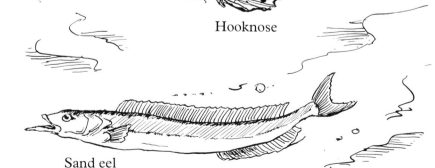

Sand eel

Useful facts

Fish cannot breathe out of the water. They have special gills which can filter air contained in the sea water.

Many fish, like the shanny, have very sharp teeth. Others, like the lesser weever, have poisonous spines. If you are in a shrimping area, wear something on your feet when you're paddling in the water. Lesser weevers burrow in the sand to catch shrimps and are very difficult to spot, so make sure you don't tread on one.

Sand eels also bury themselves in the sand, but they do this to hide from large fish and birds. You may be lucky and see a whole shoal of them darting through shallow water, looking like streaks of light.

Flat fish, like the flounder and dab, are very odd. When the baby fish hatch out from the eggs, they aren't flat at all. After a few weeks they sink to the bottom of the sea, and flatten out. The right side becomes the bottom and turns white. The left eye moves around its head until it is finally on the same side as the right eye!

A fishy word net

Can you find the following fish in this jumble?

Pollack
Dab
Flounder
Mackerel
Whiting
Shanny
Lesser weever
Sand goby
Butterfish
Sand eel

Answers on page 32

```
A S D T L I F R D A B H
P A I P S T A I O T U O
O N M A C K E R E L T S
L D O O R P I T L O T V
L E S S E R W E E V E R
A E P W H I T I N G R R
C L A T O A L S B A F T
K O F L O U N D E R I L
Y A S T O B E N A A S O
P S A N D G O B Y L H R
```

Seashore birds

Many birds live along our coastline. Some live here all the year, others only come to our shores to breed, some spend the winter here and others use the British coast as a stopover and resting point on their long journeys to other countries.

Some seabirds to spot

Lesser black-backed gull

Black-headed gull

Herring gull

Useful facts

Most gulls to not dive under water to catch their food, they snatch fish swimming close to the surface. You will often see gulls inland following a farmer's plough to pick up grubs and worms as the earth is turned over.

Kittiwakes are great travellers and spend the winter surviving the rough Atlantic storms and gales. They come to our shores in the spring to breed. Listen to this gull's call – it sounds like the bird's name – 'kittiway-eek, kittiway-eek!'.

The puffin cannot be mistaken for any other bird. It has a glorious large, red, blue, scarlet and yellow striped beak. Puffins nest in burrows to lay their single eggs. The burrows are usually dug out by the male bird, although sometimes puffins will use old rabbit holes. Puffins dive under the water and use their strong wings and webbed feet to swim when hunting for fish.

Kittiwake

Cormorant

Puffin

Guillemot

You will only see guillemots when they come to land to breed, or if they have been driven in by a storm. Otherwise they spend their whole lives at sea, resting or swimming on the water when they are not flying above it or fishing below the surface. Unfortunately, thousands of guillemots die every year when they become coated with oil spilt by ships.

The cormorant is an unusual bird. It is a very effective fisherman and either dives for fish, using its strong webbed feet, or swims along the surface until a fish comes along and then somersaults over to grab it.

A few places to watch for seashore birds

Baggy Point, Devon. The steep cliffs are useful nesting places for seashore birds such as gulls, fulmars, shags and cormorants.

Farne Islands, Northumberland. At least seventeen different species of birds use these islands, including Arctic terns, guillemots, eider ducks, puffins and kittiwakes.

Brownsea Island, Dorset. The 500-acre island has many different habitats. You may see sandwich and common terns, oystercatchers and wading birds such as curlews and redshanks.

Stackpole Head, Dyfed. The limestone cliffs are home to razorbills, guillemots, kittiwakes, puffins and choughs.

Strangford Lough, Northern Ireland. Four different types of tern nest here and 40 per cent of the world's population of pale-bellied Brent geese come to Strangford Lough in the winter.

Blakeney Point, Norfolk. This area of dunes, mudflats, saltmarshes and shingle makes a natural bird sanctuary. In spring, look out for common, sandwich and little terns, ringed plovers, oystercatchers, redshanks and sheld ducks.

Did you know?

Gulls have an efficient way of finding worms. They attract the worms to the surface by tapping the ground with their feet.

Bird jumble

Answers on page 32

The names of these seashore birds have become jumbled up. Can you sort them out?

RLEDNASNGI _____

NILUND _____

MMOOCN LULG _____

UFPFNI _____

ONENRUTST _____

UILGMLETO _____

ESLDH UKCD _____

Seashore birds

Many birds prefer to keep to the safer, shallow waters at the edge of the shore. One group of these birds is the waders. Watch them as they paddle around the water's edges, probing with their beaks for food among the seaweed, under rocks and stones.

Many ducks like to live by the seaside. The ones you are most likely to see are the sheld duck and the eider duck.

Bird watching

When you go bird watching take a note book and pencil and a camera if possible. If you recognise the bird, make a note of when you saw it, where you saw it and what it was doing. You will gradually build up a picture of the habits of that bird. If it is a migrant bird, you could try to find out where it goes to in the summer or winter and add the information to your notes.

If you don't recognise the bird, try to note its special features: the colour of its legs and beak, the markings of its plumage, the shape of its wings and tail. Don't forget that the plumage of many birds changes according to the time of year and their age. Wing tip patterns and the colour of its beak and legs are useful ways of identifying a strange bird.

Some more birds to spot

Turnstone

Fulmar

Bar-tailed godwit

Dunlin

Ringed plover

Sanderling

Oystercatcher

18

Useful facts

Winter is a great time for watching shore birds as long as you wrap up warmly. It is the time when many birds congregate on our coast in their greatest numbers. In spring they disperse to their breeding grounds. In the autumn they gradually return. Our winter visitors include bar-tailed godwits, lapwings and sanderlings.

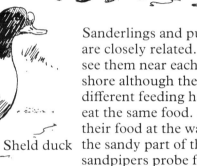

Purple sandpiper

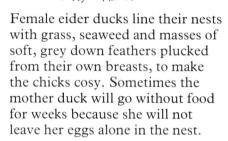

Eider duck

Female eider ducks line their nests with grass, seaweed and masses of soft, grey down feathers plucked from their own breasts, to make the chicks cosy. Sometimes the mother duck will go without food for weeks because she will not leave her eggs alone in the nest.

Sanderlings and purple sandpipers are closely related. You will often see them near each other on the shore although they have very different feeding habits and do not eat the same food. Sanderlings find their food at the water's edge on the sandy part of the beach. Purple sandpipers probe for small creatures on the seaweed-covered rocks.

Sheld duck

Sheld ducks nest in burrows, often an old rabbit hole, a fair distance from the seashore. In early summer you may catch sight of the fluffy black and white chicks being taken down to the sea for a swimming lesson.

Oystercatchers usually rest on one leg, tucking their bills under their wings.

Oystercatcher

Turnstone

Turnstones are wonderful to watch in flight. They are fast and very strong fliers, used to the strong winds of the Arctic.

Sanderlings

Remember

Many sea birds nest on high cliff edges. **Never** try to climb a cliff or go near the edge to look at a nest. You are not only putting yourself in great danger but also whoever has to come and rescue you.

If you do find a nest, do not touch it or disturb it in any way. If you find a chick away from the nest do not touch it. The parent may not be far away. If you touch a chick it will have your human scent and will be abandoned by its parents and left to die.

Marine mammals

You may be lucky enough to see some of the aquatic mammals that live around or visit our shores. Some you will only be able to see from a boat.

Otter (around estuaries)

Useful facts

Seals are aquatic mammals but, unlike whales or dolphins, they need to come on to land or ice to breed, bask in the sun and moult. They can move around on land, but they are very slow. Seals like the cooler waters of the Arctic and Antarctic and have a thick layer of fat, called blubber, under their skin to protect them from the cold.

Man has caused immense suffering to seals. They have been killed over the centuries for their fur, skins and blubber. To make matters worse, in the last few years thousands of seals have been struck by a mystery deadly virus.

Look out for:

Grey seal

Common porpoise

Common seal

Each grey seal cow gives birth to a single pup covered in soft white hair and weighing about thirteen kilogrammes. For the first three weeks of its life, the pup does little else but drink its mother's rich milk until it becomes a fat little barrel, weighing almost three times as much as it did at birth. The seal cow will then return to the sea, leaving the pup on the shore until starvation forces it to leave land in search of food.

Common dolphin

20

There are seal colonies at:
Blakeney Point, Norfolk
The Farne Islands,
Northumberland
Strangford Lough, Northern
Ireland
The Pembrokeshire Coast, South
Wales

Useful facts
Whales, dolphins and porpoises
are animals which live all their
lives in the sea. They come to the
surface to breathe and have a
blow-hole in the top of their heads
to expel used air.

They are helpless when stranded
on shore. Like all mammals, they
are warm-blooded and give birth
to live young which are suckled on
very rich milk. They are highly
intelligent animals and have a
sophisticated means of
communicating with each other.

Dangers
Man is also a great threat to
whales, dolphins and porpoises.
All of them are hunted for their
meat, oil and fat. Many dolphins
are also killed when they get
trapped in the huge nets intended
for catching tuna fish.

Seashore badges
Trace these outlines of seashore
creatures. Cut them out, stick
them on card and colour them in.
Then glue or tape safety pins on to
the back so that you and your
friends have badges to wear.

SAVE THE SEALS

DEFEND OUR DOLPHINS

The seashore at work

You may think of the seaside as a place for holiday, but it is also an important area for industry. In the past, the coast has been home to a variety of industries including slate and tin mining, fishing, shipbuilding, lime works and oil and gas production.

Fishing

From the earliest times, people who lived in settlements near the sea have caught fish to eat. Over the years, fish became more important in people's diet, especially in the Middle Ages when the Catholic Church insisted that people didn't eat meat during Lent or on Wednesdays and Fridays.

In the 1860s the use of ice to keep fish fresh meant that fishing boats could travel as far as Iceland and bring back fresh rather than salted fish. With the improvement of rail and road communications fresh fish could also be transported long distances inland.

In the 1970s the Cod War with Iceland started the decline of the deep sea fishing industry. Pollution and over-fishing added to the problem.

However, in many areas, fishing is still very important, and ports like Grimsby in Lincolnshire are flourishing centres for fish trading. There are also many small harbours, like Mullion Cove in Cornwall, all along the coastline which carry on the business of fishing as they have done for centuries. You may be able to see fishermen unloading their catch or bringing lobster pots to shore.

Some fishing ports to visit

Penberth, Cornwall is a small fishing cove with small boats which bring in lobsters, crabs and fish like mackerel and pollack caught by handlining.

Aldeburgh, Suffolk where sprats are sold from boats on the beach.

Brancaster, Norfolk with its large areas of mussel beds.

Fish cakes

Serves 4

This is an easy and tasty dish to make. Ask an adult to light the cooker.

You need:
450g filleted and skinned white fish
300 ml milk
450g potatoes, cooked and mashed
25g butter
1 egg
Salt, pepper, tablespoon of parsley

For the coating
1 beaten egg
Oil for frying
125g dried breadcrumbs
A little flour

What you do:
Put the fish and milk in a saucepan. Cook for seven minutes on a low heat. Let it cool. Strain off the milk and put it to one side. Put the fish, mashed potato, butter, beaten egg, salt, pepper and parsley in a bowl and mix. You might need to use a little of the milk to bind it together. Make the cakes by taking a tablespoon of the mixture and shape it into cakes with your (clean) hands. Sprinkle flour on both sides. Have your second beaten egg in one bowl, and the breadcrumbs on a plate. Dip each cake into the egg first and then roll in the breadcrumbs.

Pour enough oil into a frying pan to cover the bottom and place over a medium heat. When the oil is hot, put in your fishcakes, but be careful, the oil may spit when you put them in. Fry them until they are golden brown on both sides.

Delicious with tomato sauce . . .
Worcester sauce . . .

Mining

Long before the Romans came to Britain, tin mining was an important industry in Cornwall and remained so for hundreds of years. During the height of the Industrial Revolution, the tin for the South Welsh smelting works came from Cornwall.

One of the richest mining areas stretched from St Agnes to Porthtowan. About 225 million years ago, a boss of granite under St Agnes Beacon pushed up red hot from the Earth's core. The great heat and pressure affected the overlying rock, while gases and liquid forced up through cracks to form veins of silver, lead, zinc, tin and copper.

Always be careful when you are exploring and take notice of any signs which tell you to keep out. Quarries can be very dangerous.

Some quarry sites to visit
Stackpole, Pembrokeshire. The quarry is now an adventure centre but you can still see clearly the rock layers on the quarry face. Limestone was dispatched by boat from the stone pier at Stackpole Quay.

Trebarwith Strand, near Tintagel, Cornwall. The cliffs here have been used for quarrying slate for centuries. At one point, the cliff face was cut back at sea level to allow small boats to moor at its foot. This meant that the slate could be lowered directly into the boats' holds.

You will see many relics of the tin and copper industries along Cornwall's coast. Ruined engine houses perched on lonely cliff-top sites are a reminder of the times when there were 650 pumping engines working day and night in Cornwall.

Some mines in Cornwall to visit
Levant Beam Engine, Pendeen
Wheal Coates, St Agnes
East Pool and Agar mine,
Camborne

Quarries

The rock formations along the Cornish and Pembrokeshire coasts provided slate, building stone and lime. As you explore these coasts you will come across many abandoned quarries. These provide good opportunities to examine the rock stratae and to keep a look out for fossils embedded in the rock.

Danger!

Try to visit the coast on a wild, wet and windy day when the sea is dark and menacing and the cliffs and rocks look fierce and threatening.

Imagine what it must have been like out on the open sea in a sailing boat with no modern radios or radar equipment, with the rain and mist blurring your vision, and the waves drawing you closer and closer to the jagged rocks . . .

Our treacherous coast

The coast is littered with shipwrecks. One of the worst areas is the coast between Porthleven and Gunwallow in Cornwall, where dozens of ships have come to grief on the rocks. In 1527, the *St Anthony*, laden with bullion, was wrecked at Gunwalloe Cove. About 250 years later, a Spanish treasure ship was wrecked on the tip of Castle Mound and several unsuccessul attempts to recover the treasure were made, including building a tunnel underneath the seabed!

At Port-na-Spaniagh on the Giant's Causeway in Northern Ireland, you can see where one of the ships from the Spanish Armada, the *Girona*, was dashed to pieces on the rocks. Many of the items recovered from the wreck can be seen in the Ulster Museum, Belfast.

There is scarcely a mile along the Lizard coast in Cornwall that has not been the site of a wreck. In the early nineteenth century in the great days of sailing ships, the coast was patrolled twice a day, partly to try to stop smuggling but also as a safety measure.

Lighthouses

Beacons and lighthouses were built on some of the most dangerous points of the coast to warn ships of danger and to guide them to safer waters.

Ships were often drawn onto the rocks on purpose by wreckers. These evil people would light false beacons to trick the ship's captain to steer his boat on to the rocks. The boat would then be at the mercy of the looting wreckers.

Visit **South Foreland** lighthouse on the White Cliffs of Dover in Kent. This lighthouse was built in the mid-nineteenth century to guide ships through the Straits of Dover and off the Goodwin Sands – a ten-mile long sandbank known as the 'great ship swallower'. The lighthouse was only taken out of service a couple of years ago when modern technology meant that its machinery had become outdated. You can still see the two-ton turntable for the base of the revolving light.

Lundy, an island in the Bristol Channel, has three lighthouses. The oldest was built in 1820 on a high position on the island so that ships would be able to see it from near and far. Unfortunately the fogs in the Bristol Channel were so thick that the beam of the lighthouse high up on the hill couldn't be seen and ships were wrecked as a result. It was abandoned and in 1894 two replacements were built at either end of the island. This time they made sure that they were built nearer sea-level!

A white lighthouse was built on **Godrevy Island**, Cornwall to point out the dangers of swirling currents. On the day of Charles I's execution in 1649 a ship containing his wardrobe and household possessions sank off Godrevy Point.

You may have heard the story of Grace Darling. The daughter of a Northumbrian lighthouse keeper, she became a heroine overnight in 1838 by helping her father row out in treacherous storms to help rescue survivors from the *Forfarshire*, a passenger boat which had come to grief on the **Farne Islands** reefs. If you visit Wallington House, Northumberland you will see a huge painting of Grace's brave act.

Defence

Whenever you see a castle or defensive site, ask yourself the question – why was it built here?

In the case of the ancient hill forts, castles or World War II gun batteries along our coast, the answer is . . . to stop invaders.

For thousands of years, invaders and raiders have sailed across our seas: some to make lightning raids, others to conquer. Think for a moment about some of the successful invaders: the Romans, the Anglo-Saxons, the Vikings, and William the Conqueror and his Normans. And don't forget the unsuccessful attempts: the Spanish Armada, Napoleon and Hitler.

Regal Ruins

Dunseverick Castle in Northern Ireland was once the most strongly fortified place in Ireland. It was probably begun about 2,000 years ago and Conal Cearnach, leader of the Red Branch Knights – Ulster's ancient Order of Chivalry – lived here. The castle had a long and eventful life but eventually fell into decay after Cromwell's troops slighted it in the seventeenth century.

Dunstanburgh Castle, Northumberland, perched on a rocky outcrop above the sea, was built between 1313 and 1316, for Thomas, 2nd Earl of Lancaster, the grandson of Henry III. During the Wars of the Roses, in the fifteenth century, the castle was an important Lancastrian stronghold and was besieged by the Yorkists from 1462 to 1464. It was badly damaged and never repaired.

Comfy Castles

Once the danger of invasion had passed, some of these formidable fortresses were turned into comfortable homes.

Perched on top of a crag on Holy Island, Northumberland, is **Lindisfarne Castle**. It was built in 1548 on the order of Henry VIII to defend the harbour from possible French invaders. Much of the stone used to build the castle came from the island's Benedictine monastery which had been dissolved by Henry in 1537.

From the outside, Lindisfarne still looks like an impregnable stronghold, but inside it has been converted into a snug, comfortable home. In 1900, Lindisfarne's owner, Edward Hudson, asked the famous architect, Edwin Lutyens, to transform the castle into a home without destroying its character.

St Michael's Mount, Cornwall is one of the most memorable homes and castles in England. The Benedictine priory was turned into a formidable fortress in 1425 and remained so for the next two hundred years. In the mid-seventeenth century the castle was bought by the St Aubyn family (who still live there) and converted into a comfortable home. Have a look at the bollards around the island's harbour. Some of them are made from the barrels of old guns left over from the times of the Napoleonic wars in the nineteenth century.

War Flame

In the early fourteenth century, during the struggle between Edward II and his French queen, a warning system was set up in England so that if any enemy ships were sighted, the news could quickly spread throughout the land.

A chain of beacons was set up so that the warning could be passed on by the sign of lighted bonfires on the summits of hills. By the end of the fourteenth century there were hundreds of beacons throughout the country, many of which were permanent structures of tall oak posts with iron braziers filled with inflammable material. At the time of the Spanish Armada in 1588, the beacon chains were a vital part of England's defence plan and played an important role in warning troops and the navy of the approach of the Spanish fleet.

Beacons are still lit nowadays, but usually to celebrate national events rather than to warn people of danger.

Find a map of the area you are visiting and discover where the beacons used to be. Try to visit a beacon site so you can get an idea of the planning behind this effective warning system.

Other defensive sites to visit

The Needles Old Battery, Isle of Wight was built by Lord Palmerston's government to defend the south coast from a possible French invasion in 1861. You can see the wrought iron guns from the 1870s and the gun powder magazine.

Brownsea Island, Dorset was thrust into the forefront of national affairs during Henry VIII's reign in the sixteenth century. When Henry declared himself Head of the Church in England, he angered all the Catholic countries of Europe and prepared to defend England against invasion. Poole had developed into a thriving port and Brownsea Island was the town's first line of defence. The merchants of Poole petitioned Henry to join with them in building a fortification to guard the deepwater channel, just inside the harbour entrance. This blockhouse is now the heart of a 'mock' castle built by the island's owner, Sir Humphrey Sturt, in 1765.

Smugglers

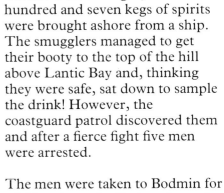

Britain's coast has the perfect recipe for smugglers: secret coves, hidden beaches, caves, and close to France and Ireland.

For hundreds of years, rum, brandy, salt and many other goods were smuggled ashore in the dead of night, avoiding the watchful eyes of the revenue officers. Cornwall, Devon, Lundy, East Sussex and South Pembrokeshire were all great smuggling areas. There are thousands of smuggling tales . . .

King of the smugglers

A hundred and fifty years ago Manorbier, Swanlake, New Quay and Bullslaughter Bay in South Pembrokeshire were the favourite haunts for people smuggling goods into Wales. Under the cover of darkness, brandy or rum could be transferred from a French vessel into the smuggler's rowing boats. It would be taken to the shore and hidden – in a cave at New Quay, in a cellar at Swanlake or down an ancient well at Manorbier Castle.

The 'King of the Smugglers' was a man called William Truscott, who often came into conflict with the revenue officers. He had many narrow escapes but usually managed to outwit his pursuers. However, in 1834, during one of these raids, Truscott was caught red-handed at New Quay. He ran, but as he was trying to escape across the water to Pembroke Dock, he was shot by a revenue officer, and drowned.

The fight at Lantic Bay

In October 1835, the last great conflict between coastguards and smugglers on the Cornish coast took place at Lantic Bay. At the time, this part of the coast, east of Fowey, was not well guarded and local smugglers took great advantage of the situation!

On this October night, one hundred and seven kegs of spirits were brought ashore from a ship. The smugglers managed to get their booty to the top of the hill above Lantic Bay and, thinking they were safe, sat down to sample the drink! However, the coastguard patrol discovered them and after a fierce fight five men were arrested.

The men were taken to Bodmin for trial but instead of being charged with smuggling they were put on trial for felony (a serious crime). The jury found them not guilty and the judge had to set them free because they hadn't actually been charged with smuggling.

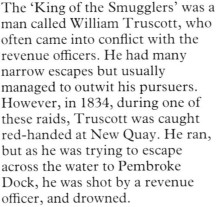

As a result of this, a watch house was built at Lantivet Bay, and a detachment of coastguards was permanently located there, making life very difficult for smugglers! You can still see the cave at Lantic Bay where smugglers used to hide their goods.

A salty tale

During the late eighteenth century, salt was heavily taxed and the poor suffered greatly because of this. Salt was important, not only as a flavouring, but also as a preservative for food.

One day a spy informed the Justice at Solva, South Pembrokeshire, that a vessel had come in with smuggled salt aboard. The Justice sympathised with the poor and didn't want to convict the smugglers in this case, and so came slowly down the hill to the coast, roaring at the top of his voice 'I'll punish the rascals! They shan't thieve from his most gracious Majesty, my beloved King. I'll salt the devils!'

Those in the boat below heard every word, as the Justice had intended, and had time to hide the salt from the view. By the time the Justice reached the boat to inspect it, no salt was to be found.

Smugglers' tales

Whenever you visit the coast, especially in the areas mentioned, ask the people who live there about smugglers. You will be told all sorts of tales – some true, and some made-up. Write them down and make your own book of Smugglers' Tales.

Look out for clues to smuggling. For example, at Rye, East Sussex, many of the old houses have huge cellars said to be linked by secret passages. At Ogof Mwy, near St David's in Dyfed, if you look carefully, you will see a flight of steps carved into the cliff face. These are said to lead to a tunnel to a nearby mansion!

Seaside holidays

If you and your family want to visit the seaside for the day, or for a holiday, you jump in the car, or onto a coach, or catch the train. It is only in the last hundred years or so that travelling long distances has been so easy with the development of railways and roads.

Seaside holidays became fashionable in the late eighteenth century when people thought that bathing and drinking sea-water was good for you. However it was only the rich who could afford the money and time to travel to the exclusive seaside resorts. This all changed in the mid-nineteenth century when the railways developed, providing cheap and quick transport for everyone. This led to the growth of popular seaside resorts like Harrogate and Blackpool with theatres, amusement piers and Punch and Judy shows.

However, if you don't like the hustle and bustle of busy seaside résorts and want to find a quiet, beautiful beach, there are still many undeveloped stretches of seashore around the coast waiting to be explored.

Some National Trust beaches to visit

Cornwall
Pendower Beach
Poldhu Cove
Strangles Beach

Dorset
Studland Bay

Devon
Branscombe
Wembury Bay

Merseyside
Formby

Norfolk
Brancaster Straithe

Northern Ireland
Whitepark Bay

Northumberland
Druridge Bay
St Aidan's Dunes

Somerset
Porlock Bay

Sussex
Birling Gap

Suffolk
Dunwich Heath

Wales
Barafundle
Newgale
Mwnt

Yorkshire
Cayton Bay

Pollution

Investigating the Seashore is an introduction to the magic of the seashore. The National Trust is desperately trying to keep the spell unbroken, but one of the main dangers to this magical world is pollution. Once the National Trust owns a stretch of seashore it protects it as well as it can: it manages the area with expert staff, it protects the area from development and clears away litter washed up on shore or left by untidy visitors. However, it is powerless against preventing major disasters at sea which cause pollution.

In recent years the seas have become polluted with oil spillages, untreated sewage, rubbish and other waste, resulting in the deaths of thousands of sea birds, mammals, fish and causing great harm to marine life. You just have to see a picture of a sea bird covered in oil to understand the destructive force of pollution.

Although you can do little yourself to stop major pollution disasters you *can* do your bit to save our shores from litter pollution. **Never** leave any rubbish on the beach. Apart from spoiling the beach's beauty, litter is dangerous to bird and wildlife who will often eat it by mistake, thinking it is food. Seagulls, who are scavenging birds, can die from food poisoning if they eat rotting food left behind by unthinking visitors. Birds and animals can also damage themselves by getting tangled up with litter left on the beach. So remember, take your litter home with you!

Answers

Page 10
Who made these marks in the sand?
1. Sand casts and hollows of lug worms
2. Gull tracks
3. Paw prints left by a dog

Page 15
Fishy Word Web

```
A S D T L I F R D A B H
P A I P S T A I O T U O
O N M A C K E R E L T S
L D O O R P I T L O T V
L E S S E R W E E V E R
A E P W H I T I N G R R
C L A T O A L S B A F T
K O F L O U N D E R I L
Y A S T O B E N A A S O
P S A N D G O B Y L H R
```

Page 17
Bird jumble

Sanderling
Dunlin
Common gull
Puffin
Turnstone
Guillemot
Sheld duck

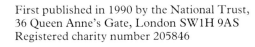

First published in 1990 by the National Trust,
36 Queen Anne's Gate, London SW1H 9AS
Registered charity number 205846

Text and illustrations © The National Trust

ISBN 0 7078 0110 9
Designed by Roger Warham, Blade Communications
Phototypeset by Southern Positives and Negatives (SPAN), Lingfield, Surrey (7548)
Printed in England by BPCC Paulton Books